Contents

Introduction 3

Make money as a writer 7

Make money on blog and website 30

Make money on Instagram 35

Make Money Taking Pictures and Taking Photos 42

Make Moneyto Currency ExchangeatHome 47

Make money on the stock exchange and alternative investments 54

Make Money on Youtube 61

Make money on a podcast 75

Make money by renting out your home online 80

Make Money From Home Online

More and more people are attracted by the opportunity to **make money from home**. Being able to quickly bring in some extra income in your spare time is something that you want to be able to do for various reasons. You may want to pay off some debts, save up for a cash bet, car, or for that dream trip that you have so long wanted to go on.

Whatever the reason, there are now many opportunities to withdraw some extra money. The development of technology has also made it easier than ever to make money online. This means that there are good opportunities to make money from home - or to be able to work exactly wherever you want.

Furthermore, by **making money online** you can set your own schedule and work when it suits your own lifestyle. In this way, it is not a problem that you have a lot of times to fit in, but it is even very good to combine a regular full-time job with making extra money from home.

Why Should you Make Money in Addition to your Work

There are many reasons why it can be good to make extra money. With rising living costs and a wage trend that in many cases is difficult to keep up with, it can be very positive to earn some extra money in addition to their work.

Even if you already have a high standard of living, extra income can be a way to get that extra gold edge on life that you might not be able to afford otherwise. By making money in addition to their work, you also have the opportunity to increase their savings. Then you can quickly get enough money together to be able to buy, for example, your dream home - or the car you so much want.

If you are in the position that you have already been able to buy everything that you dream of, you can instead save to build a greater financial security. **Maybe you even want to be able to retire early ?**

Create a Safer Private Economy

A larger saving can mean that you build up capital that gives you a greater opportunity to cope with financial setbacks. Longer illnesses or redundancies at work and more are things that are difficult to predict - but which can have a significant negative impact on the private economy.

If you have had a larger saving in such a situation, you do not need to feel as stressed about the economy. Just that in itself can be very worthwhile.

Can Give you a Golden Edge on Life

But whether you want to save more or consume more, extra income is very positive for one's private finances. Many of us have quite large costs every month. You may have an expensive accommodation, a car that costs a lot of money, or many children to provide. This makes it easy to spend quite a lot of money.

It may even be that most of the salary usually goes for a regular month. In this way, extra income can be a very good addition to the economy. Money that you earn in addition to your regular salary is a bonus that can be added either directly to the savings, or to be able to buy something you want or need.

Make Money as Writer From Home

Are you good at expressing yourself in writing? Do you need extra income, maybe a job online that you can perform remotely? Then an extra freelance writer may be something for you!

But how do you get started as a freelance writer? Can you really make any money from it? How much does one make of writing texts? In this article, we go through everything you need to know to make money as a freelance writer.

Where can you find a job as a writer?

There are several ways to go about trying to make money from writing texts. To make it easy to understand, we could divide it into a couple of categories:

- freelance Platforms
- Companies that hire freelancers
- Find your own customers who demand your services

Freelance Platforms - Part of the gig economy

There are a number of large international platforms where customers can look for freelancers who perform the services they seek, and where freelancers can advertise their services. Three of the largest and most well-known such platforms are:

- Fiverr
- Freelancer.com
- Upwork

Fiverr is a platform that has grown relatively large in a relatively short time. From the start, a lot of different jobs were offered that could be done for $ 5 - hence the name Fiverr. The site has since become a major platform with freelancers and clients spread all over the world performing all kinds of services, from logo design for $ 5, to complete music productions for thousands of dollars. Fiverr's range has an extremely wide range, both in terms of services and prices.

When it comes to writers, there is a relatively large selection of freelancers, as well as customers, especially when it comes to texts in English,

A big advantage of Fiverr, for both customers and freelancers, is that it is very easy to order services on the platform. It basically works like in an online store where you click on the "item" you want, pay for and wait for delivery. The advantages

and dis advantages of Fiverr as a freelancer could be summarized as follows:

advantages:

- **Easy to register and start working** - It's very low threshold to get started on Fiverr. Everyone can apply and get started, which is not the case on all similar sites.

- **Easy to get a job** - Once you've laid out your jobs, it usually doesn't take too long for people to find you and you get your first job.

- **Easy Payments** - Although it takes a few weeks from the time the job is completed, the payouts work smoothly.

- **Good app** - Thanks to a well-functioning app, it is easy to quickly communicate with customers even if you are not "in the office".

Cons:

- **High fee** - Fiverr charges quite high fees. 20% of the amount you charge for your services. In addition, they charge a small fee even on the purchase side. In addition to this, they are almost a bit reluctant to encourage buyers to leave after work, which of course they charge a service fee.

- **Rogue players** - Because it's so easy to register and get
- Started on Fiverr, there are a lot of rogue players. It happens that people copy other freelancers' presentations straight off, steal design or the like. Sometimes there are rude
- Requests, suggestions that limit illegal activities or spam comments. However, Fiverr is relatively good at clearing and blocking users who behave inappropriately, but some are slipping through.
- **Customers with a lower budget** - Since Fiverr has a background as a platform where various services are sold very cheaply, there is a tendency for customers to have a lower willingness to pay. However, it is you yourself who set the prices in the end and since a united state writer does not have to compete against, for example, freelancers from Asia or the like, the same fierce competition that it can do in other industries does not arise.

Freelancer.com is another great platform for freelancers in a variety of professional categories. Freelancers' model is based on the fact that those who need help with a service can

Outsource a project and so freelancers can participate in bidding for the project according to what price they consider reasonable to work for. At Freelancer there are smart features

That allow you to get paid for parts of your work, so as not to risk payment missing after a large part has already been done.

A negative thing with Freelancer, compared to Fiverr is that it is more difficult to register, and the process of getting started and working is more complicated. Here are some pros and cons of Freelancer.com as a platform for freelance writers:

advantages:

- **Big company** - Freelancer.com has been around for a long time, they have customers all over the world and are experienced in the freelance industry.

- **Many potential customers** - With Freelancer you have the potential to reach a large number of customers and many large companies have hired freelancers through the platform.

Cons:

- **High fees** - On services, fees can be up to 20%, on projects they can be slightly lower.

- **Difficult to get started** - It is a lengthy process to apply and you may not be accepted with your application to work at Freelancer.com.

- **Other Fees** - Freelancer charges some other fees, in addition to percentages on your work. They encourage employees to upgrade to "premium accounts" in order to reach customers better, they charge high exchange rates between currencies and also charge for accounts that have been inactive for a certain period of time.

Upwork is another very large platform created to connect freelancers with customers who demand services in a variety of industries and occupational categories. The platform has more in common with Freelancer.com than with Fiverr and the assignments are often awarded through bidding, where freelancers are allowed to bid on different assignments. At Upwork, work is usually paid per hour, which differs from, for example, Fiverr where it is usually paid per work done according to agreement.

At Upwork, just like Freelancer, it is somewhat more complicated to apply for a job. On the one hand, you are judged on the basis of your experience and qualifications, as well as on how the offer looks for the services you want to offer. Since texts in World are not a huge part of what is sold at Upwork, there is a relatively small space for writers who want to write texts in english.

Advantages and disadvantages of Upwork as a freelance platform:

Benefits

- **Experience** - Upwork has been around for many years and is a large and well-known platform that houses many freelancers around the world.

- **Serious impression** - Upwork has a very professional appearance and attracts many serious entrepreneurs. It also

- Means that many freelancers can pay reasonably for their services, even though prices are squeezed by bidding, which is often found on projects at Upwork.

- **Secure payments** - It is quick and safe to get paid for work done at Upwork.

Drawbacks

- **Threshold to enter** - Upwork makes an assessment of your qualifications and the extent to which your services are in demand.

- **High fees** - Like other platforms, Upwork has charged high fees. However, they become lower the more you earn, which is a good incentive to keep working, even if it results in you earning less in the beginning.

- **Extra fees** - Upwork has special member services where you have to pay to get better opportunities to find jobs.

In addition to these three major freelance sites, there are a plethora of other platforms, some more niche in specific industries, or towards certain markets, others more general. Below is a list of a variety of sites for freelancers of different kinds.

When it comes to foreign sites, there are almost as many

Writers who want to write in English. On the sites we list here there is the opportunity to offer services.

- Top figures - Premium service with very selective admission process.

- Guru - Freelance platform for all possible professional categories.

- PeoplePerHour - A platform similar to Fiverr a bit close to the program, but with less activity.

- Simplyhired - Recruitment platform with a lot of distance jobs, such as freelance writer jobs.

- Hiroy - Platform for competence in digital services, from content to technical jobs.

- Whereuare - Mediator of services that can be performed remotely.

- Web jobs - Different types of web jobs.

- Brainville - Consultant assignments for consultants, many assignments to suit different types of freelancers including writers.

- Indeed - Great platform for employment services. By

- searching for jobs that can be done from home, you can

- Sometimes find a lot of jobs that suit freelance writers.

- LinkedIn - On LinkedIn you can search for "remote" jobs, ie jobs that are performed remotely. There are usually a relatively large number of available jobs in various occupational categories, including writer jobs on and off.

- Okelii - A platform for project-based employment services. Has some activity and is free to use, but the membership can also be upgraded to a PRO membership.

One disadvantage that is common to many of the freelance platforms is the high fees. Freelance platforms are a great way to get started as a freelancer, but can get expensive in the long run as the fees eat up a fairly large portion of the cake over time.

At the same time, they are a great way to find jobs you would otherwise not have come into contact with. The freedom to set the price for your work and work based on your own premises is a great advantage of the profession and it is definitely worth trying some of these platforms to see if it is something for you.

Companies that hire freelancers, there are many companies that offer text content for companies and websites, so-called content agencies. These are often used by freelance writers, unless they have their own team of writer's in-house or permanent staff remotely. One way to find a freelance job can thus be to apply to this type of agency. Some examples of companies that hire freelance writers are:

- Boostcontent - Large content agency offering content and translations in many different languages.

- Contentor - Another great content agency that employs many freelancers.

- Copypanthers - Translation and content, offers its customers everything from blog texts, to SEO content and more.

- Stockholm Writing Agency - Stockholm-based content agency with a database where you can register as a freelancer to be matched with any jobs that fit your profile.

These were just a few potential employers for you who want to make money from home writing. There are many companies engaged in producing content and you can always contact the companies to check the needs of the services you can offer.

Find your own customers who demand your services

One way to get around the fees charged by the freelance platforms, or by content agencies, is to find customers yourself and start a collaboration. This page is one of my ways to potentially be seen by customers who want to hire a freelance writer. If you have a website, blog or similar, you can advertise your services there.

You can also try contacting companies or other websites that publish a lot of written content. It doesn't cost anything to ask if someone needs help with content, but you have to be prepared that it can be time consuming and involve some work before you find your own customers.

There are several benefits to working entirely on your own and managing customer contact yourself:

- **Payments** - You decide for yourself how you want to be paid, what price you should take and ultimately keep all the profit after tax.

- **Terms** - You set your own terms and conditions and meet customers based on your requirements and guidelines. By building a direct relationship with your customers, you have the opportunity to have good long-term partnerships without external pressure or opinions from employers.

- **Independence** - You do not depend on a particular platform but stand on your own legs. If you go through another company or platform for freelancers, your destiny lies in their hands and your future becomes a little more uncertain.

However, there is no denying that there are several negative aspects that come with your decision to stand on your own:

- **Difficult to get a job** - Freelance platforms and content agencies charge a fee for a reason, they put a lot of resources into being visible and building trust with customers. When you stand on your own legs you must instead strive to find work, nothing falls into your knees by itself.

- **Uncertainty** - There is a certain risk of being a freelancer and self-employed. If you deliver a job and do not get paid, you must take up the fight yourself to get paid. This risk is significantly less with a larger company in the back, which usually pays in advance and holds the money until the work is completed.

- **Greater responsibility** - When you are self-employed you are responsible for everything. Payments are handled, you keep your own deadlines, manage customer contacts and have to find your own jobs. It means some extra jobs to stay afloat and be able to work as a freelance writer without any support from a company or platform to stand on.

However, one positive thing about being a freelancer is that you do not have to choose just one employer, or one way to find

Clients. You can advantageously try to find and look for customers both through freelance platforms, content agencies and by going out on your own to find customers.

Do you need a lot of experience to work as a writer online?

No. In fact, you don't have to have any experience at all to get started really. But of course, all relevant experience is valuable to succeed in your work as a freelance writer online. Of course, you need to have a good habit of the written word in the language you want to work with. Being a freelance writer is potentially a very good job for students who have time over and are used to writing a lot in connection with their studies.

Some employers place higher demands on you as a writer and want you to have experience and certain specialized knowledge in various areas to hire you. But many freelance platforms, for example, do not require anything special, but it is up to the

Customers to decide if they want to hire you. The more satisfied customers you have, the more jobs you will see that you get, so it is important to make sure you deliver well to increase their chances of making money as a freelancer.

How Much Can You Make From Writing Texts Online?

How much you can earn from working as a freelance writer varies depending on a variety of factors, such as:

- Experience
- How fast you write
- Your reputation
- The relationship with your customers
- How to pay

An inexperienced writer should be able to achieve at least $ 100-200 per hour before tax within a reasonably short time. A more experienced writer with a good reputation and serious clients should be able to achieve at least double that. Of course, there are writers who earn more than that, but these levels are within the scope of what is reasonable to expect.

But as a freelancer, it varies quite a bit from mission to mission how much you can earn. If you pay per word, some jobs can result in a low hourly wage if they are more time-consuming than you expected, while others go really fast and become profitable if, for example, they are in an industry you are familiar with.

Should you as a freelancer pay per hour or a fixed sum for his work?

In the case of freelancers who live on writing texts, it is relatively common for the payment to be made at a fixed price per word, but hourly pay also exists. There are both advantages and disadvantages to both these payment models, for both the writer and the customer who order the job.

A price based on the number of words provides an incentive for you as a writer to be effective. You focus on your assignment and do your best to get the job done as quickly as possible. The disadvantage from the client's perspective is that it also provides an incentive for you to fill in the text with more words, even though they do not increase the value of the content.

If the price is instead paid per hour, as a writer you have an incentive to fill the text with quality and carefully review your text to see that it is correct, relevant and has good content. From the customer's perspective, there is instead an obvious risk that the time required for writing will be longer and the price will be more expensive per word.

When it comes to the quality of the text, it is up to you as a writer to live up to the client's expectations, no matter what

Payment model you use. It is a matter of taste which way you want to be paid and it can be good to be flexible according to the customer's wishes. With experience, you will then learn which model suits you best and what works for you.

For whom is it suitable to work as a freelance writer?

To be able to work as a freelance writer, it is good if you have an easy time for writing, master the writing language well and actually think that writing is fun. For example, being a writer is suitable for you as:

- Want an extra income in addition to your regular employment
- Am a student with a lot of time left
- Want to be able to make money online and work remotely
- Want an extra nap while working on your own projects
- Want to live as a digital nomad

Trying to get some writing jobs is the best way to find out if it's something for you. A fun thing about the job is that you learn a lot along the way. Everything from general education in all the areas you get to write about, to specialized skills such as SEO, content marketing, or writing texts for the web.

A few things to think about if you are going to work as a freelance writer

It's very easy to get started and make your own money online by working as a freelance writer. There are a few things that you may want to consider before you get started:

- **Tax** - When you make money as a freelancer, you have to pay taxes on your income. For example, if you bill directly to a customer, you can use one of the many solutions available for private individuals to invoice without business . In other cases, you should check for yourself and make sure you pay the right tax on your income.

- **Time** - As a freelancer, you are responsible for ensuring that your job is delivered on time. You should have good preparation and plan your life so that you have time to do the jobs you take on.

- **Accessibility** - As a freelance writer you have a lot of freedom, but you should still be available for contact with customers. By being able to respond quickly to inquiries, a good relationship with customers is maintained, which creates confidence and conditions for future collaborations.

Summary

Being a freelance writer is an easy and fast way to get started and make money on the internet. It provides a great deal of freedom and is a job that can be done remotely, anytime and almost anywhere.

There are several good ways to find jobs, but one of the easiest is to start by going through a freelance platform.

Whether you are looking for a new career, or just want an extra income in addition to another job, a freelance writer can be something for you. It doesn't cost anything to try, so give it a try if you think it sounds interesting!

Make Money on Your Website

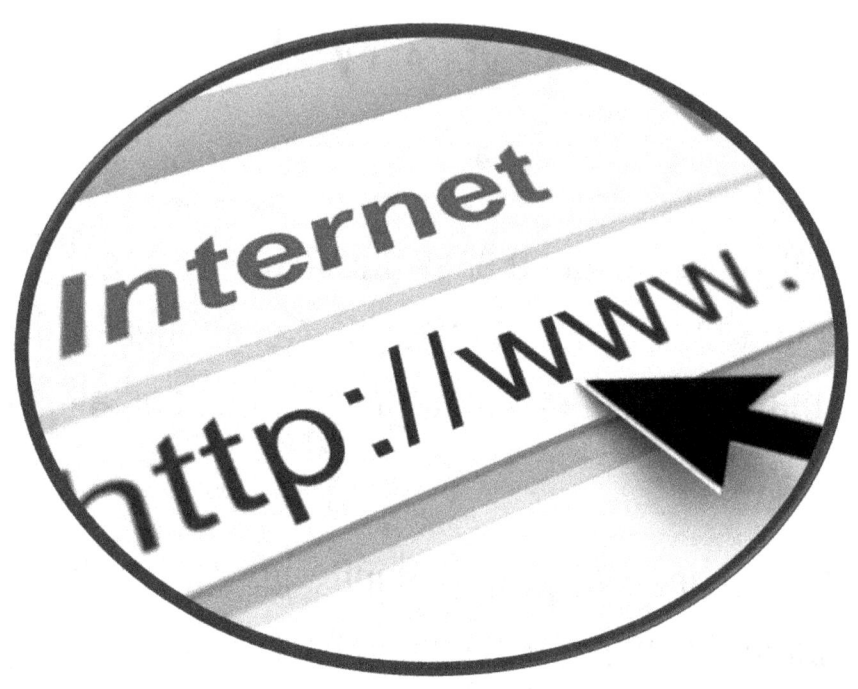

Learn how to create a website for yourself or your business. We show you how to create it and make money on your website.

Start planning your own website:

1. **Which site?** Should it be a personal blog, an online store, a website for your business, an online service, or a forum? Find out what kind of website you want!

2. **Functionality?** Do you want to be able to post news with pictures, do you want a contact form, forum, an intranet, an admin panel where you can edit your page? Find out functionality for your site.

3. **What you need to create website:**

   1. **You need**

   - domain
   - Web hosting
   - a computer with internet connection (of course)

   2. **Buy domain and hosting**

   Hosting and domains are cheap today. We recommend that you use Bluehost for hosting (web hosting) then you will get domain free.

   3. **In the domain name**

   Quite simply, a domain name is the address of your website. It is the name that people type into the URL bar of their browser to find your website. Domain names can be purchased through a domain registrar or through your hosting provider. They are also often provided for free by hosting companies or website builders. Using the domain name xxxx.com is an international domain.

4. Cheapest Web Hosting

It depends on what you are looking for, but with Bluehost you get free domain when you buy web hosting, and they have a very good hosting service!

TIP! Don't use free web hosting. It is almost always never wise to invest in a free domain and web hosting solution. You only wonder if you think you have a better solution for free. No matter how big or small you imagine your site to be, then you've earned paying for my own domain (costing under 100 dollar of the year) and hosting (which is something everyone can afford). Don't waste time trying to find free options, there are no effective solutions that are free - all free solutions for blogs, forums and websites have major drawbacks, and believe us when we say you will regret later if you choose free web hosting and "free domain" (read: you only get a negligible subdomain, and never a real domain if you choose something for free).

How to create your own website:

There are many ways to start creating websites, some are much easier and better for people than others.
Creating Website Even the Easy Way (Recommended): Use Bluehost is one of the best equipped solutions for those who want to create their own website / website, blog, forum, online services and other online solutions. You do not need the help of a web developer or programmer, it is easy to do even if you use Bluehost. You simply click on the solution you want, such as a Traditional website or a WordPress blog or a ready-made website and then install it on your website - in your own domain that you get with Bluehost. You can scale and change your website exactly how you want it.

The difficult way to create the site (not recommended) is to learn a server language side programming like PHP or ASP, as well as XML, CSS, XHTML, web design and everything else – and

Then add started building the page. People think they can learn this in a day or a week. In reality, it takes several years to become good at creating websites and writing functional code.

Amateurish way of creating website (not recommended) is to use a "home program", like FrontPage or other programs. You will probably end up with a very incomplete and amateurish performance and a website with no functionality. Also, choosing this solution will make it harder to update the page.

Therefore, the best way to create pages and services online is to use **this website softweare from Bluehost**. It's cheap, easy and you can do it yourself with just a few mouse clicks, write your name on the page and create content. The technical solution is ready already, and you do not need expertise to create the site.

Now you know everything you need to get started with creating professional websites - without having to pay a web developer to do this for you. It's easy, fast, cheap and above all, fun to do it on your own. You also get a website that is just the way you want it.

Make money on Instagram

Making money on Instagram has recently established itself as one of the most

Ways to make money on the internet. Young girls and guys who barely turned 20 earn many thousands of dollars by posting pictures advertising various products.

How is it possible to earn so much on Instagram?

Well, suppose you have 10,000 followers and start a collaboration with the company X that wants to market a product that costs 500 dollar.

You post the picture with the product and 500 of your followers make a purchase. Company X has now earned 500 × 500 = 250,000 dollars your remuneration for marketing the product amounts to 10, 000 dollar, which in this context is small money. Now imagine that you have 100,000 followers or more, it will quickly become big money. So many followers are the key to success.

Everyone can make money on Instagram

As you know, Instagram is a free service where anyone can register. This means that anyone can also make money on Instagram. However, be aware that it is a relatively small number that really succeed.

If you aim to be big on Instagram then the hard work applies. The big money is found in areas such as fashion and beauty, but here too the competition is brutal.

At first it may be worthwhile to niche in a smaller area.

A good tip I can give you is to subscribe to subcategories like party dresses or sports shoes. If you focus on special products, chances are you will succeed.

However, it must be an area that the followers are interested in so you get more followers.

If you want to succeed on Instagram, you have many followers. Here are a few tips you can use to gain more followers,

- Be active and post new pictures at regular intervals.
- Make sure the pictures posted are of high quality.
- Use relevant hash tags to help other users your images more easily.
- Reply to comments and comment yourself on others.
- Post your photos on other social media sites like Facebook and Google+.
- There are several sites online where you can buy followers for your Instagram account, avoid these.

Your files Represents and the images you post represent your brand,

And that you have to be afraid of. Buying followers can seem attractive, but in the long run it can have negative consequences.

Focus on quality before quantity Just as Just like the first two points above describe, it is important to be active and publish qualitative pictures to gain more followers. You should post at least 1-2 new photos every day, but only post pictures that you are happy with yourself. If you focus solely on quantity, you risk losing followers.

As you gain more followers, you will also get to know your audience better. With Services such as AgoraPulse, you gain access to important information such as the time of day that is best suited for publication and the type of images your followers appreciate.

Tips from the big protocols

When you do a Google search on "Make money on Instagram" you get thousands of hits. Most of the results are interviews with the big names on Instagram where they tell how they succeeded. Interestingly, it is a tip that often comes back - the social part.

Instagram is a social forum where members comment on each other's photos. So you have to give in order to get, tell your followers about other protocols on Instagram whose pictures you like. Also write comments and give praise, so you get more followers yourself.

Make money on Instagram through collaborations

As described further up the page, everyone can make money on Instagram. If you have an account with many followers, you can start collaborations with companies in your niche and publish pictures with advertising for products. The more followers, the higher the compensation you get for each campaign.

Initially, you can expect to hunt for companies to partner with yourself.

Introduce yourself, your protocols on Instagram and describe what kind of followers you have. If the company in question it's interesting and rewarding to start a collaboration with you, it is a good starting point.

If you become so large that the companies themselves hear about it, it can be worthwhile to hire an agency. They help you with everything from agreements to pricing, which facilitates and gives you time to work on other fronts.

The importance of niche

Many of the big names on Instagram appear in popular areas such as fashion,

Health and beauty. However, one should be aware that these protocols have worked for several years to become large. Since these categories are so popular, it is difficult to settle in as a newcomer, therefore it may be worthwhile to start in a smaller area.

No matter which direction you choose to work with, there is a red thread running through the ones that images are published. In the long run, it is of great importance when you start collaborations with companies because they want to know what interests your followers have.

Summary

In order to make money on Instagram, you have to get a lot of followers. Post new photos regularly, but make sure the photos are of high quality. Don't you think you are not there, other social media like Facebook and Pinterest can work as a good complement?

As you gain more followers, you can start your own collaborations with companies within your niche and post pictures of specific goods or products.

However, be sure to protect your followers, it will not be popular if you use too many advertising images.

I often repeat that it takes time to succeed and this is especially true of Instagram, you have to give it time and accept that nothing happens overnight.

You Can Make Money Taking Pictures and Taking Photos

Here is a good opportunity to make money. Not many people know about this and it's a shame, because there are many who could make some money here.

Anyone can make money selling the image online. You can be a professional photographer, amateur photographer or beginner, it doesn't matter.

What NOT to do: You do not need a professional camera to begin with. You also don't have to have your own website, or make other major investments.

What you need: All you need is a digital camera, internet access, and knowledge of how to effectively make money from their photos.

What you need to do is take pictures with your digital camera and add these pictures to image databases on the Internet. An automated process is also possible.

Earn 150,000 dollars a week

Proof: Check out all popular image databases online, see how many downloads the best photographers have, and multiply the number of downloads by commission revenue per download.

This is a lucrative industry! Even amateurs who have relatively few downloads can earn well.

It really isn't that hard to make money on this, but there are some tricks and tips you should know before you get started. We will not go into detail on this, but recommend **DigiCamCash** as useful information and inspiration.

How to make money selling the image online?

What you need to do is send your digital pictures in image

databases on the Internet. Probably there are thousands of such image databases on the Internet. It is possible to automate the process of uploading, this is one of the many tricks that make it easier to make money online pictures.

Where should you send your photos?

There are many places to publish images, and all serious image databases pay their photographers. There are thousands of image databases, here's a guide that shows you **how to make money from your images** .

Who buys the Pictures?

When the pictures have been published, someone wants to buy the picture ... Photos are sold in image databases and can be

Used in many contexts, eg. In newspapers, on websites, in ads, blogs and so on.

What you buy is actually a license (or rights) to use your image in your own material. As a rule, anyone who buys the photo can use it freely, without credit to the photographer.

How much money can you make in a photo?

When someone downloads a photo, you will earn a commission. Some image databases pay a lump sum per image, but most depend on commission.

You will be paid based on how many downloads the image has and what size they download the image in. Small images cost less than high resolution images. You get one percent for each seal, which varies from 10% to 90%, again depending on the type of database you are using.

Examples of how much you can earn

Let's say you take a photo of the Riksdagshuset in Stockholm, and published this picture in a photo database. In one year you have 125 downloads of the image. For each download, you earn an average of $ 35, and you've earned $ 4,755 - just in this picture. If you publish the image in other image databases as well, you can earn even more.

If you sell more pictures you can make a lot of money. Don't forget that you will be able to make money from the photos as long as they are in the photo database, and usually they will be

Available there for several years.

Let's say you manage to publish 50 images a month image databases on the Internet. In one year, you have 600 photos online. Some pictures will give you a lot of money, and others will not provide as good income. But if you earn an average of only $ 250 a year on each image, you are left with an income of $ 150,000.

If you only earn $ 100 on each image, but publish 500 new images each month (6,000 in one year), you want to get an income of 6,000 x 100 which is $ 600,000.

The biggest secret to making money from selling photos is (as you can see from the example above) to publish as many images in as many image databases as possible online. By automating this and following the tips in **this photo guide**, you will be able to make good money from selling the image on the Internet.

Make Money to Currency Exchange at Home

Forex trading, involves trading in different currencies. When trading in currencies, trading is done in so-called currency pairs. Forex traders try to make money speculating on the value of one currency compared to another currency in a currency pair.

The usual major currency pairs traded on the world market are:

- EUR / USD
- AUD / USD
- USD / CAD
- USD / JPY
- USD / CHF
- GBP / USD

How does currency trading work?

If you want to trade in currencies, you do so through a forex broker. There are many different brokers on the market and it is good to look around a bit before deciding which broker you want to use. Currency trading includes certain fees that are good to keep track of and these may vary somewhat between the different brokers.

Spread - When you trade in currency, there is a so-called spread, a difference between the prices of buy and sell for each currency pair. The spread can change and differ between different currency pairs. It is important that the spread is low in order for you to have a chance to make money in foreign exchange trading.

Brokerage - Sometimes a brokerage is added, a fee to open and close a position. Just as when it comes to stock trading, the prices for brokerage can vary widely between different brokers.

Slippage - Sometimes the broker will not be able to process your order for the bid you have made, for example to end your position. Typically, there will be greater slippage during volatile periods, for example, when news releases affect the rapidly moving market. A good broker should usually make sure that your order goes through at the next best price, as soon as possible in order to minimize the slippage cost.

Trade in currency

To trade, you first need to decide which currency pair you want to trade with. In the currency pair there is a so-called base currency and a counter currency. If we take the example EUR / USD, EUR is calculated as the base currency, since it is stated first in the currency pair.

A common way to trade in currency is through so-called CFD trading. This means that trading is done through derivatives, which can often be traded for leverage. By trading with these products you speculate on the up or down of the underlying asset, but technically you are never the owner of the currency

Itself. By using leverage, you can take a larger position through a smaller sum without having to cover the entire position directly. You only pay the amount required to cover the security requirement of the broker. However, if your position goes in the wrong direction, you risk losing the entire amount, so it is important to understand the product before you trade it, in order to keep track of the risks.

When dealing with a currency pair, you can choose to go either long or short. This means that you are speculating on either the rise or fall of the currency pair. When you trade in currency, it works like buying the base currency while selling the counter currency. But it may be easier to imagine the currency pair as a whole unit instead. Then it works like this:

- If you buy EUR / USD you are going long the currency pair and hope that the euro will go up in value against the dollar
- If you sell EUR / USD, you are going short of the currency pair and hope that the dollar will go up in value against the euro.

Trade with a strategy

To succeed in currency trading, you should have a predetermined strategy. It is important to have patience, discipline and to set clear rules for your trade. You should consider how much leverage your capital allows you to trade,

and always have clear stop loss rules for yourself.
One starting point is to take small positions, max any percentage of your trading capital should be risked every time you want to take a trade.

Study and learn from your mistakes
To learn currency trading and be successful, you need a plan for how to develop. There are many books and courses where you can learn basic knowledge as well as more advanced forex trading strategies.

Be sure to write down your thoughts and document every trade you make so that you can learn from your mistakes. Sometimes experience is the only way to develop, and in trading there are few things that beat experience.

Benefits of currency trading
One advantage of currency trading is that it takes place in the world's most traded market. Every day, multibillion amounts are traded on the international currency market. The market is open 24 hours a day, five days a week.

Another advantage of currency trading is that it is very easy to get started and try. No huge sums are required to get started and take their first trades. Start with very small positions so you learn how it works and see if it's something for you.

Disadvantages of currency trading

One disadvantage of currency trading is that it is very difficult to predict how the market is moving. It happens a lot all the time and it can often feel like currency prices are moving completely randomly one moment, and then react very strongly to various news.

Another disadvantage of currency trading is that there is an abundance of spam-like content online where people want to sell courses, or attract people to rogue brokers.

Some tips for those who want to try currency trading

Currency trading is generally considered to be difficult to succeed. At the same time, it is easy to get started and it is a very accessible market. Here are some tips for those who want to start currency trading:

Just deposit money you are ready to lose

If you trade in leverage, a bad position can become expensive very quickly. Put yourself at risk and only trade with money you are ready to lose.

Use stop loss and set up rules for your trade

You should have a clear plan for each trade, both for potential downside and for the upside. In order for your strategy to work in the long run, you need to know when to sell to maximize profits and when to take the stops to avoid excessive losses. It is important to see currency trading as a long-term game where the goal is to be successful over months and years, and not to believe that you have to be successful in every single trade.

Be patient

The easily accessible market means that many beginners are very eager and want to enter new trades all the time. It is wise instead to be patient and ask yourself about a possible trade why exactly you think you have an edge in that trade. What kind of signal has caused you to want to go into a position right there? If you want to become proficient in currency trading, you should be able to answer that question when you want to enter the market and take a position.

Reverse theory with practice

If you want to become better at currency trading you will need to both read and translate what you learn in practice. You will need to learn to recognize and take advantage of situations that arise in the market. You must quit your job if you want to become one

Make Money on the Stock Exchange and Alternative Investments

There are two primary ways you can make money on stocks. The first option is to sell your shares at a higher price than what you bought them for.

The other alternative is stock dividends. This means that you get to take advantage of the company's profits that are paid out to the shareholders.

1. Sell the shares at a higher price than what you bought them for

Another way to get a return on a stock investment is to **sell the stock at a higher price than you bought it for**. This requires thorough analysis of both the companies and the market as a whole.

Here the term "index" is good to know. Index counts the trend in most different stocks and can therefore serve as a comparative figure. There are many different indexes you can use.

The most common index is what is called OMXSPI where the value of all shares listed on the Stockholm Stock Exchange is weighed together. This index therefore provides a good overall picture of developments on the stock market in general. Similar indexes exist for all other exchanges.

But an index can also weigh in on how the share price in a particular industry has changed over time - if you want to invest in a company in the clothing industry, the index development for that industry can provide important information while you can see if the company you are interested in has historically been above or below index.

2. Dividend distribution

One way in the long term to get a return on a share investment is through a dividend where a portion of the profit is distributed among all shareholders. Thus, it is the number of shares you own that determines how much of any dividend you are entitled to.

How much is distributed in relation to the share price is called direct return - the higher direct return a company has, the more dividends you receive per share. Not all companies offer dividends to their partners. It is usually the larger, more mature companies that have high and stable profits that distribute money.

Smaller companies rarely have the opportunity to pay dividends, but instead need to invest their profits in the development of the company. Remember that in the event of a dividend, money is transferred from the company to the shareholders, which means that it remains less in the company. Read more about **dividend shares** and **investment companies** that are very good beginner shares.

You can vote for or against a possible dividend

A decision on dividends is made at the Annual General Meeting and you as the owner are always entitled to participate in this. The Annual General Meeting usually takes place once a year. The more shares you own, the more votes you have at the AGM and the greater the opportunity to influence the company's future.

The AGM is, of course, voluntary for shareholders, but if you have invested in companies you are interested in, it can be a good opportunity to both get information and at the same time have an opportunity to influence the company's future direction.

What are key ratios and which ones should be known?

Other important concepts to know in order to make a relevant analysis are P / E numbers and P / S numbers. P / E is an abbreviation for "price / earnings" and is one of the most important key figures for assessing what price a share is worth. **Read more about key figures** .

The P / E ratio shows the price per share in relation to the company's earnings per share and can therefore not be calculated if the company loses. Earnings per share are calculated on the total profit divided by the total number of shares. When trying to decide whether to buy a stock at the current price, the P / E ratio can be useful as it shows whether the market (the stock buyers) values the company high or low.

P / S figures, which stand for "price / sales", instead show the share price in relation to the company's turnover, or sales.

This figure, just like the P / E figure, gives an indication of how the market values the company. Unlike P / E, P / S can be calculated even in companies that are at a loss, which can be quite common for smaller companies.

The P / E and P / S figures are good indications, but it is not always obvious that a company that is already highly valued by the market is a good investment, a low-valued company that you believe has good prospects can generate significantly higher returns over time.

Large companies usually offer lower and more stable returns

Generally speaking, large companies with many shareholders are more stable and less flexible. This gives less risk while limiting the potential for big profits.

Smaller companies that are rarely traded have a greater fluctuation in the share price, which means greater growth potential in the long run. Much of the ups and downs on the stock exchange are about pure speculation and expectations of the companies' profit development.

There are many psychological factors that play a role and an expected rise or fall can create a snowball effect as investors do not want to lose money or miss a possible increase in value.

Save monthly, spread the risks by owning several companies and being long-term

Trying to dot the tops and lows of stock trading is therefore almost impossible but here it is about spreading the risks and investing in companies that you have confidence in in the long term.

Create a portfolio with a wide variety of companies from different industries and sizes. A combination of stable dividend shares combined with smaller growth companies is usually a good starting point. See equity investments as long-term savings rather than quick money.

Do not invest too aggressively and do not invest money that you will need in the near future without investing money you can save for a long time. It is important to remember that a gain or loss on stock trading is not realized before selling your shares.

It can be emotionally stressful to see their investments decrease in value, but the best thing to do purely financially when the stock market is swaying is to sit quietly in the boat. Once you have chosen an investment strategy, it is always best to stick to it even at a downside as the stock market usually yields returns in the long run, even if it is at times negative.

Make Money on Youtube Step by Step Guide

Do you dream of becoming the next star on Youtube? Want to make money creating videos about your interests? Here is a guide to how to get started and what it takes to succeed.

A first relevant question is whether there is any point in investing in becoming a Youtuber? Is there a future there? Today, many point to the fact that Youtube will largely replace traditional television viewing.

Recent statistics show that the use of Youtube continues to increase. 85 percent of all worlds' internet users have ever watched Youtube. It is significantly more than just a few years ago.

But what is more important is that the use among young people

is extremely high:
Youtube gets bigger with future generations, in other words, it is not unjustified to say that Youtube will continue to grow (and become even more commercial) as future generations change. For those who are growing up today, Youtube and Social Media are obvious sources of visual consumption. And there is nothing to suggest that this will diminish - on the contrary.So yes, there are absolutely great opportunities to support yourself, even get really rich, if you invest in becoming a Youtuber.

To give you some inspiration, let's start by looking at some Youtebrs who have succeeded extremely well with this.

4 Examples of Extremely successful Youtubers

1. PewDiePie

Citizen, known by his alias PewDiePie, is not only most famous Youtuber in Country, but the whole world (in terms of the number of subscribers), currently his channel has over 62 million subscribers.

PewDiePie began his career on Youtube by commenting on action and horror games, but over the years he expanded his repertoire by commenting on all sorts of games.In recent years he has moved away from the game commentary and is now creating significantly "broader" content. This way, one can rather call PewDiePie entertainer or comedian than gamer

2. Roomie

Joel "Roomie» broke through and became a viral superhit with the YT video "One guy 14 voices" where Joel imitates 14 famous artists and songs.

Since then, Joel has published lots of similar videos on his Youtube channel "Roomie".

The content is similar to the success video with imitations, but now Joel also makes his own songs and comics / entertainment on his channel. Currently, Roomie has 3.5 million subscribers.

3. RobTopGames

This Youtube channel has about 3.3 million subscribers at the time of writing. RobTopGames is a purely "gamer channel" run by Robert Topala, Swedish game developer.

On the channel, Robert publishes relatively short videos with excerpts from his own games.

In this way, the channel does not produce very much unique

content, but rather acts as a marketing platform for the games. The frequency of publications is not particularly intense: last year Robert has just posted five new videos on the channel.

But Robert certainly makes a lot of dough. Two years ago, DI wrote an article about how much money "Spelundret fra Upplands Väsby" raised:

"Do you know the game developer Robert Topala? You should do that. His company Robtop Games raised over 82 million dollar US last year - with a profit margin close to 97 percent. "

4. Family Playlab

The Yoube channel Family Playlab is a good example of making money on Youtube - and getting many subscribers - in a very narrow niche.

The channel was started a couple of years ago by toddler dad Tomas Hellberg, and publishes videos in which Tomas films his children's experiences of different play countries.

Nowadays, the content has been expanded to include waterland, but the basic concept is still the same.

Currently, the channel has 2.5 million subscribers, and has become something of a power factor and Influencer in "children's TV" and children's experiences.

3 Different Ways to Get Paid on Youtube

1. Make money with Google Adsense ads

Google owns Youtube. This means that Google will be your "employer" if you want to make money from ads that appear directly in your videos.

To get started, you first need to reach Google's minimum requirements for a commercial Youtube channel.

Now, the requirements became stricter than before, and now means that your content must be approved by Google, and your channel must have at least 1000 subscribers and get at least 4000 viewing hours in a year.

If you meet the requirements then you need:

1. Review and agree to the terms of the YouTube Partner Program
2. Sign up for Google Adsense

3. Make monetization settings

4. Get reviewed (your content is reviewed and verified by Google)

Once you've gone through this process, Google's algorithm will place ads in your videos that suit your target audience.

So you do not need to do any manual advertising, but this is then (almost) handled completely automatically.

2. Make Money with Affiliate Marketing

This is an alternative way that many smaller channels and actors use.

The strategy here is to create videos that rank on Google and then link in the text content to an affiliate product.

This way you can get commission if someone clicks on the link and converts. To learn more about how affiliate marketing works,

3. Make Money as Influencer

Making money on Youtube as an Influencer means that you enter into your own advertising agreements with companies and get paid in this way.

In other words, the company will pay for mentioning or placing their products / brands in your videos. Think "product placement" as a business model.

New, and tougher, guidelines since January 2018

After several controversies over the past few years, where well-known You-tubers have expressed themselves as inappropriate and provocative (according to Google's guidelines), Google decided to tighten the requirements on who publishes content - and what content may ... yes, contain.

Among other things, those guidelines mean that Google raises the bar on the number of impressions and subscribers you need to make money. But also a tighter control of the content itself.

Here's how Google writes about the new guidelines on its website:

Youtube (only) becomes a channel for "big" brands?

As it seems right now, it seems to be very difficult for small channels to make money on Youtube. For example, statistics show 99% of those affected by the new guidelines earned under $ 100 last year through Google Adsense.

Most of these small players will probably not meet the new requirements of 4000 viewing hours and 1000 subscribers. Then they would probably have earned more than $ 100.

To clarify. The rules apply only to getting paid on Youtube through Google Adsense. So even if you do not meet the requirements, you can still make money from, for example, affiliate links or as Influencer.

The trend, on the other hand, seems to be that Google will from now on release major brands on Youtube.

The new guidelines will also create higher thresholds to get you started as a commercial Youtuber at all.

2 Alternative ways to make money on Youtube (marketing strategy or enhancement)

1. Marketing strategy for companies

As an entrepreneur you can use Youtube to get more visitors to your website or e-shop. Here are lots of opportunities to be creative and create
interesting, fun content.

Here are 6 tips from Drive-eget.se about how you as an entrepreneur succeed on Youtube:

1. Think about content promise!
- Present to your followers what they can expect for material on your channel. This can be done, for example, through a channel trailer, ie a commercial for what the viewers can expect.

2. Set a publishing strategy!
- How often will you upload content once a week or every two months? Be continuous and realistic!

3. Be patient and think long term!
- A successful Youtube channel does not build overnight.

4. Listen to your customers!
- Use the opportunity to have an ongoing dialogue through the comments on your videos.

5. Take the help of the experts!
- Look at those who are already good on Youtube, channels with many viewers can help drive traffic to your channel.

6. Create personal content!

- Youtube is character driven, so make content that is personal and that fits the platform, for example shorter videos are more popular than longer.

2. Reinforce already popular channel

If you are active in another social channel, such as running a podcast or publishing music, you can use Youtube to reach more people with your content.

In this case, Youtube will not become your primary channel, but more as a platform for sharing your content and driving traffic.

3 Steps to get started with your own YT channel

1. Choose theme and target audience (what are you passionate about?)

"Content is king" is a term that is often used to describe. The same goes for Youtube.

To be successful, you need to create videos that engage. Who gets shared, commented - that arouses interest.

PewDiePie became successful by commenting on games, Roomie's ability to imitate known song voices, Family Playlab through its unique way of filming children's experiences of playland.

One tip is to choose a theme that you are already genuinely interested in. Ideally something you are really passionate about.

Why? To make it so much easier to create content then. And that genuine commitment and passion is hard to fake.

(After all, it will not be particularly fun to create hundreds of videos within a theme that you are not particularly interested in.)

So start by deciding the theme of your channel and which target audience you should turn to. Also consider if the theme is commercially viable.

If you are really interested in the anatomy of the Mongolian dung beetle then it may not be an interest you can make money from (although you should never say never…)

Large, commercially viable niches on Youtube are, for example:

- Fashion
- Food
- Sport
- Beauty
- music
- Funny

2. Select format (possibly invest in new film equipment)

Part of the challenge is of course to create good videos. Videos that do the content justice with good image and sound. Sure, you can safely film with a regular mobile phone. But the result will be then.

In order to achieve a more professional result, you will need to invest a good deal in new film equipment. And in any software where you can edit your videos.

3. Create the channel and spread the message

Once you have decided on the theme and got the hang of how to create good videos, it's time to register your own Youtube channel and start publishing videos.

Once all these basics are in place, it's time to promote your channel.

The basic thing is that you publish at least one video a week. That way, those who already like your channel will occasionally return to see if you have created any new content.

And already there you have laid a good foundation for constant traffic.

Other ways to promote your videos are

- Advertise in the Google Ad Network on Youtube
  By advertising in the Google Ad Network on Youtube, your videos can be seen in the stream that Youtube relates to your content, as well as in the "Coming Next" feed. But also as a link in other relevant videos. This is a very effective and still relatively inexpensive way to get traffic and viewers to your videos.

- Comment on other videos within the same theme
  If, for example, you have created a channel with content that is mainly about Italian cooking, it is a good idea to find other channels with the same theme and comment on them.

What is most important? (Start with this!)

The most important thing if you want to make money on Youtube is that you get started and record videos with interesting and engaging content. So if you're going to start with one thing - start there.

Make money on a podcast

The article series is based on almost three years of experience as a pod producer and seller in the pod industry. During the fall we will compile more experiences from our daily work with podcast sales and share what we experience.

Facts of life - the rules of the pod sphere

Already in the nineties, your only chance was to reach out with something you created through student radio or Open Channel.

But in these media very few people listened or watched. If you did not hit the producers on the lip, the road to success was closed.

But in the name of honesty, it was, after all to enter the fine rooms of the production companies and the TV channels or radio stations required contacts, luck or a discovered talent and the needle eye was minimal.

But today! Today, anyone can start a YouTube channel or podcast. You can reach millions of people in just a few hours. And heck, the problem is the other way around. Everyone wants to reach out.

But as a pod maker, it's really one big some may be abandoned for a long time. Others may broadcast a few times a year, but the number of world podcasts will soon be up to half

Fantastic you might think problems why? Just because everyone can do the same thing as you. And that they actually do. So how do you make your podcast appear slightly higher in the pod heaven than everyone else's? The answer is not easy but we will try to do what we can to give you what you need.

The myth of breaking through the noise

Since I am also active in the app industry, I join several Facebook groups where you can get help with their app idea. Just recently someone had asked what the most difficult thing about building an app was. There were 6 response options.

In place number one came the expense of the app, building an app is certainly not easy, but today there are actually WordPress-like tools that can do it for you. You can also use offshore companies (where I run one, among other things) to bring the price down to levels your local office can contribute without even having to take out a loan.

In place number two came "income during the time you build the app". If you think this is a problem, you should probably not

Enter the app world at all. I think you should consider both once and twice if you want to become your own entrepreneur and run your app idea if you can't solve that bit. The reality for an entrepreneur is that it takes one or more years before you make a profit, but there is a superstition on app technology today - a bit like the nineties with their web pages.

In place number three came marketing. People who have app ideas believe most seriously that just because they release their app it will hit. The Appstore has over 16 million apps today. None of the people I spoke to have any marketing plans for how to get on the Appstore listings (which is a great way to get downloaded). In much the same way, many people seem to reason about their podcasts.

What do I need to reach?

We can punch holes in a myth directly: "I can live on my podcast only it gets big enough". Absolutely! If you are famous. And hardly then. What you can do is make money on your podcast as an extra income. There are, of course, exceptions to this rule, but after almost three years in the industry with fairly good insight into the pod sphere, I would say that the opportunity to make money on the pod is still not very big.

Podcasters employees work to have a better impact and thus also a more monetary opportunity. In another article, we will address the issues surrounding the marketing industry and podcasts, which is probably so exciting. If you're not familiar, a few things are required for advertisers to find your podcast interesting.

You need at least about **10-15000 listeners** No rule without exceptions but this is the reality today.

Reaching that level usually requires your pod to be niche,

This is because there is no interest in the pod audience to listen to two unknown people who have opinions on things. Aim at a special topic you know well and make sure there are many people out there who care about the topic. You can be as good as you like, but if you don't have an audience it doesn't matter and that leads us to the next point:

It takes commitment to listen Reading a blog is easy. You can do this on your mobile phone, toad or computer. It takes a few seconds to skim the preamble and then read on or skip the post. A podcast requires headphones that you actively launch the pod and get past the vignette before it gets started and it is often necessary to listen for several minutes before deciding if

This is worth listening to. In order to catch the listener

An engaging topic (and how do you know that the listener cares about your topic) is required, as well as knowledge of dramaturgy and also sound editing to create an interesting environment. Just recording and dropping without thinking about dramaturgy, content, quality and more is to shoot itself in the foot and maybe also the reason why many podcasts go to the grave after three episodes.

Lastly, we assume you want people to listen to your podcast whether you make money on it or not. If your goal is to make money, I suggest you get a job or continue on what you have in the first place and see the pod as a possible small source of income. But to get there you need to have listeners and it requires marketing.

Make money by renting out your home online

Horror stories about vandalized apartments and brothel activities in conjunction with rentals have become everyday news. The figures show that renting out can pose great risks if you are not on your guard. With services such as AirBnb, more and more People have been lured by being able to make money from renting out their home but do not realize how devastating the consequences can be. Don't take unnecessary risks when renting - we've listed the best tips on how to make money & avoid problems when renting out your home.

Are you thinking of renting out? With the rent calculator you can safely and easily calculate what you can profit from renting out your home in the other.

As more and more people are looking at the opportunity to make money from renting out their home when, for periods of time, you do not need the space, not only does the market increase but also the problems that arise. In addition to increased uncertainty, it also attracts many rogue players in the market. Renting their home in the other hand can in many cases be compatible with great risks - and if you are not on your guard, it can lead to devastating consequences. According to Housing Agency, over 50% percent of problems are associated with renting out their home in the alternative, which is a worryingly high figure.

But calm down we help you! Many of the most common problems that arise are easy to avoid. Here we have listed **our 5 most valuable tips** that minimize your risk of being hit for future problems with your rental.

1. Apply for a permit

To legally rent out your home, you need permission from your condominium association or landlord. This is a basic premise! If you rent out your apartment without a permit, you risk not being able to follow up if any damage or problems arise during your rental period - you have a hard time claiming your right if you rented out illegally! Make sure you apply for a permit well in advance before you intend to rent.

2. Document the apartment carefully before entering

Before handing over, you should, together with your tenant, go through the apartment thoroughly before handing over the property. Establish an inspection record of the property's condition and a hot tip is to take many pictures and possibly even film around the home. As the burden of proof lies on you as a landlord, accurate documentation can be very important to

You should a conflict arise afterwards? However, it is important to keep in mind that your tenant must return your home in its original condition, but normal wear and tear may occur. Create an inventory list and note any damage or defects.

3. Establish a proper contract

Be sure to draw up a written lease signed by both parties. You and your tenant must have access to each copy. Feel free to use a contract specifically tailored to second-hand rentals so you don't miss important details. It is important to state in the contract which rental you have agreed on and if you rent out a rental right you should also write that the rent should follow the rental development. If the rent is increased over time, the secondary rent shall also be adjusted accordingly.

4. Take a reasonable rent

It can feel tempting to take a high rent to make extra money on your rental, but according to the rental law, the rent must be reasonable. What counts as reasonable rent differs between condominiums and rental properties. If you take too high rent for your rent, you may in the worst case become retroactive to repayment and also need to lower future rents.

If you own a condominium, your tenant can apply for reduced rents on future rents if your rental proves to be unreasonable.

Is my rent really reasonable? Check out and read more about what counts as reasonable rent here.

5. Ask for credit information

As a private person, you have the right to request a credit report for yourself once a year free of charge. Therefore, please ask your potential tenant to take a credit report to rule out that he has no previous payment notes. If your potential tenant does not want this, it can be difficult to trust that they will actually pay their bills on time. Be extra vigilant with a tenant who does not want to provide credit information!

Do you think this seems complicated to keep track of yourself?

You can take advantage of the help of an intermediary who helps you and makes sure everything goes right before, during and after the rental period.